DEMCO

Looking at . . .
Velociraptor
A Dinosaur from the CRETACEOUS Period

THE NEW
DINOSAUR
COLLECTION

**For a free color catalog describing Gareth Stevens' list of high-quality books,
call 1-800-542-2595 (USA) or 1-800-461-9120 (Canada).
Gareth Stevens' Fax: (414) 225-0377.**

Library of Congress Cataloging-in-Publication Data

Amery, Heather.
  Looking at-- Velociraptor/written by Heather Amery; illustrated by Tony Gibbons.
    p. cm.-- (The New dinosaur collection)
  Includes index.
  ISBN 0-8368-1087-2
  1. Velociraptor--Juvenile literature. [1. Velociraptor. 2. Dinosaurs.] I. Gibbons, Tony, ill.
II. Title. III. Series.
QE862.S3A447 1994
567.9'7--dc20   93-37064

This North American edition first published in 1994 by
Gareth Stevens Publishing
1555 North RiverCenter Drive, Suite 201
Milwaukee, Wisconsin 53212 USA

This U.S. edition © 1994 by Gareth Stevens, Inc. Created with original © 1993 by
Quartz Editorial Services, Premier House, 112 Station Road, Edgware HA8 7AQ U.K.

Consultant: Dr. David Norman, Director of the Sedgwick Museum of Geology,
University of Cambridge, England.

Additional artwork by Clare Heronneau.

Printed in the United States of America

 3 4 5 6 7 8 9 98 97 96 95

Looking at . . .
Velociraptor
A Dinosaur from the CRETACEOUS Period

by Heather Amery

Illustrated by Tony Gibbons

THE NEW
DINOSAUR
COLLECTION

Gareth Stevens Publishing
MILWAUKEE

Contents

Introducing Velociraptor

Velociraptor (VEL-AH-SI-RAP-TOR) was a small but very fierce dinosaur that lived about 90 million years ago in the part of the world now called Mongolia. This was during the Late Cretaceous Period.

Velociraptor's name means "speedy robber." It ran around on two long legs, chasing mammals and other small dinosaurs, then attacking and killing them with its sharp claws.

This dinosaur's remains were first brought back to the United States by scientists who had been on an expedition to central Asia.

Velociraptor can be easily recognized by its low, narrow head and the sicklelike claw on each hind foot.

Were many dinosaurs able to fight off this predator or escape from its greedy jaws? How do scientists know what it looked like and how it lived? You can find the answers to these and many other questions in this book.

Swift predator

Velociraptor was about as tall and long as a large dog. It had a lightweight body and could run very fast.

Its arms were long and thin but strong. On each hand were three clawed fingers. When racing through the forests or across the plains on its two legs, Velociraptor held up its muscular tail for balance.

Most remarkable were the two giant claws that Velociraptor had on its feet. Countless prey must have yelped in pain when stabbed by these.

At the end of its long neck, Velociraptor had a small head with a long, flat snout. Its narrow jaws had about 30 sharp, curved teeth that sloped backward.

Velociraptor's jaws had strong muscles for biting and tearing off chunks of meat.

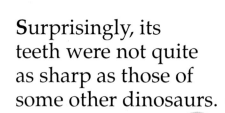

Surprisingly, its teeth were not quite as sharp as those of some other dinosaurs.

The nostrils on the front of **Velociraptor**'s snout were large. This may have given it a good sense of smell to sniff out food. **Velociraptor** would turn its head to catch the scent of its victim on the wind.

Velociraptor killed and ate other small dinosaurs, as well as their eggs and babies. They also ate small mammals and hunted in packs.

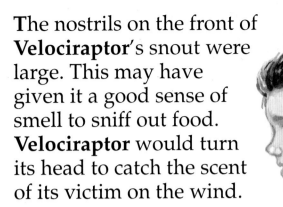

Scientists think that **Velociraptor**'s skin was probably scaly and tough. No one knows for sure what color it was.

Velociraptor's arms were short compared to its legs. These long, slim back legs helped make **Velociraptor** a fast runner and successful predator when chasing smaller herbivores.

You would have found it impossible to keep up with **Velociraptor**, even on roller skates!

Velociraptor's eyes were quite large for such a small head, which probably meant it could spot its prey at a distance.

Built for hunting

Because its bones were lightweight, **Velociraptor** could run quickly on its two back legs when chasing prey for a meal.

Velociraptor's tail was very special. Most of the tail bones were surrounded by long, bony rods that allowed **Velociraptor** to hold its tail very stiff when running. This helped **Velociraptor** keep its balance when going at great speed.

Velociraptor also had versatile neck muscles and could twist its head easily when searching for a victim.

Its long skull had many spaces in it, which made it light. The skull had large holes for eyes and also for the nostrils on top of its long, flat snout. Scientists believe **Velociraptor** was almost always on the prowl.

It may also have swung its tail to one side when changing direction or turning a corner while tearing through the forests.

Velociraptor probably used its tail to balance itself when attacking. This way, it could claw more easily at some unfortunate dinosaur.

Velociraptor had very strong shoulder muscles. These muscles gave power to its small arms so it could grasp its prey even more viciously.

Velociraptor would flick the longest claws forward to slash its prey.

There were just three fingers on **Velociraptor**'s small hands — but any creatures it chased had to beware of its finger-claws, too! **Velociraptor** could grasp firmly with its fingers, using them like hooks. Together with its athletic legs, these fingers helped make **Velociraptor** a good hunter.

Its jaws would snap shut on any prey very quickly, too, and its bite was powerful once a victim had been caught. Few creatures would have managed to escape once **Velociraptor** had them in its grasp.

Velociraptor probably used only two of its toes for running. All four toes ended in sharp claws. The biggest claws must have looked very threatening to all sorts of Cretaceous creatures that were at risk of being attacked.

Velociraptor was not nearly as huge as **Tyrannosaurus rex** (TIE-<u>RAN</u>-OH-<u>SAW</u>-RUS <u>RECKS</u>), but it was still one of the most dreaded killers of the dinosaur age. As you turn the pages in this book, you can see just how incredible it looked.

Desert life

Velociraptor lived in the area that is now the Gobi Desert in Mongolia. Today, the Gobi is a dry, cold, and windy plain, covered with stones and just a few plants.

Other dinosaurs lived alongside **Velociraptor**. Among them were herds of **Protoceratops** (PRO-TOE-SER-A-TOPS) that roamed across the plains searching for juicy plants to eat.

But when Velociraptor lived there about 90 million years ago, the weather was much warmer and wetter.

These dinosaurs laid their eggs in nests. They had to guard these eggs and any newly hatched babies against hungry, meat-eating dinosaurs.

Avimimus (AV-I-<u>MIME</u>-US) was a small dinosaur that looked very much like a bird. It had a short head with a toothless beak, two long legs, and pointed claws on its toes. Its short arms may have had feathers on them, but **Avimimus** could not fly.

Although **Ankylosaurids** ate plants and did not attack other dinosaurs, they could put up a good fight against **Velociraptor** by swiping it with their tail-clubs.

Ankylosaurids (AN-<u>KY</u>-LO-<u>SAW</u>-RIDS) were dinosaurs with thick, armored bodies and bony heads. They also had bony clubs at the end of their tails.

Fast movers

Some dinosaurs were enormous and plodded heavily along on all four legs. Other dinosaurs, such as **Velociraptor (1)**, were built for speed. They were small and light and ran quickly on their two long legs.

Some of these fast-moving dinosaurs, such as **Struthiomimus** (STROOTH-EE-OH-MIME-US) **(2)**, ate only plants and used their speed to escape from hungry predators.

But others, like **Velociraptor**, used their speed to hunt prey.

One of the fastest dinosaurs was **Hypsilophodon** (HIP-SEE-LOAF-OH-DON) **(3)**. It ate plants and may have been able to run at speeds up to 28 miles (45 kilometers) per hour. Remains of this dinosaur have been found in southern England.

Scientists determine how fast a dinosaur ran by measuring the length of its legs. Then, they compare this figure with the length of the legs of animals alive today.

1

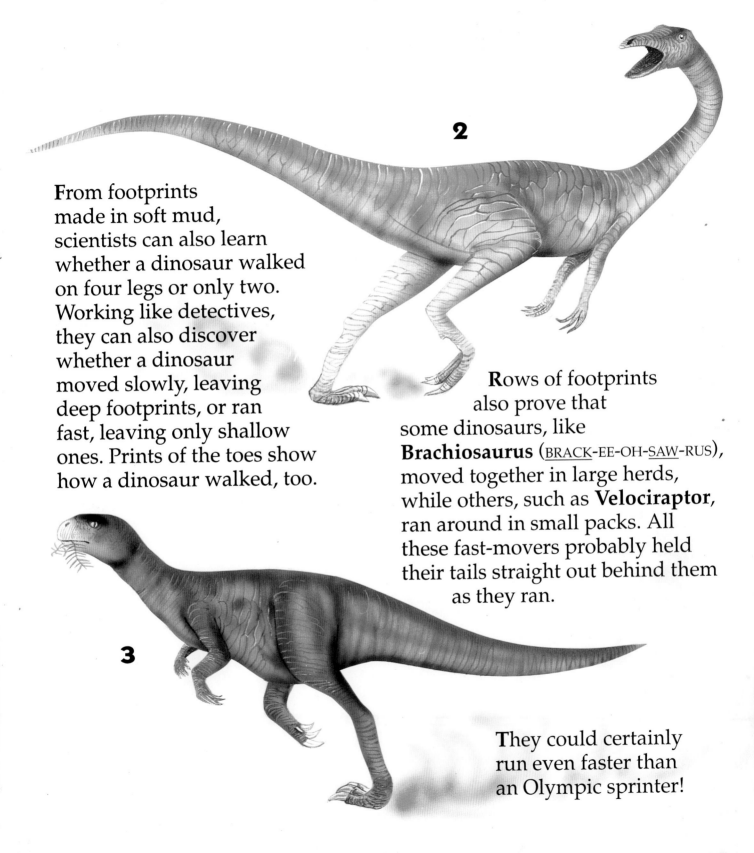

2

From footprints made in soft mud, scientists can also learn whether a dinosaur walked on four legs or only two. Working like detectives, they can also discover whether a dinosaur moved slowly, leaving deep footprints, or ran fast, leaving only shallow ones. Prints of the toes show how a dinosaur walked, too.

Rows of footprints also prove that some dinosaurs, like **Brachiosaurus** (<u>BRACK</u>-EE-OH-<u>SAW</u>-RUS), moved together in large herds, while others, such as **Velociraptor**, ran around in small packs. All these fast-movers probably held their tails straight out behind them as they ran.

3

They could certainly run even faster than an Olympic sprinter!

Bloodthirsty hunters

An **Ankylosaurid** was grazing on plants growing on the banks of a shallow lake. It plodded along slowly, pulling off leaves with its

Danger lurked! The **Velociraptor** were hungry and on the prowl.

beaked mouth. It was enjoying a good meal, unaware that nearby, among the trees near the lake, was a small pack of **Velociraptor**.

Suddenly, the **Velociraptor** spotted the **Ankylosaurid**. They raced toward it, grunting loudly. They quickly spread out so they could attack the **Pinacosaurus** on all sides at once. It would make a delicious dinner.

The biggest **Velociraptor** leapt toward the **Ankylosaurid**'s head, trying to grip it with its front claws.

The **Ankylosaurid** lunged toward its attackers, butting at them with its bony head.

Again and again, other **Velociraptor** attacked, tearing at the soft flesh of the **Ankylosaurid**'s belly. The **Ankylosaurid** butted with its head and gave great swiping blows with its tail-club. But its enemies moved too quickly. The lone **Ankylosaurid** did not stand a chance.

Another **Velociraptor** sank its teeth into the big dinosaur's back leg. The **Ankylosaurid** lashed its tail. The bony club on the end thumped against the **Velociraptor**'s thin leg, breaking the leg with a crack. The wounded dinosaur screamed and dragged itself away.

The battle was soon over. The **Ankylosaurid** lay dying in the mud, and the **Velociraptor** closed in to begin their feast, biting into their victim's body. Other dinosaurs were safe . . . until the **Velociraptor** got hungry again.

15

Fight to the death

Bones of a **Velociraptor** were first found in 1924, but scientists knew little about it at first. Then, about 25 years ago, a group of Polish scientists made one of the most exciting dinosaur discoveries ever.

They were on an expedition in the Gobi Desert when they came across the fossilized skeleton of a **Velociraptor** mixed with the bones of a plant-eating **Protoceratops**. What had brought them together?

The two dinosaurs were about the same size, but **Protoceratops** had a thick, bulky body and a bony frill around its neck. It seemed that **Velociraptor** had been holding the bony frill with its front legs, kicking at **Protoceratops**'s soft belly with the claws on its legs.

Protoceratops had probably tried to defend itself by butting with its head and by biting its enemy's chest with its mouth.

The two dinosaurs must have killed each other and died at almost the same moment. Locked together, their bones became fossilized as a record of a fight that happened millions of years ago.

No one knows why the fight first started. **Protoceratops** was quite a large, well-armored dinosaur for **Velociraptor** to attack and kill. But the struggle may have begun when **Velociraptor** was caught stealing eggs or babies, and the angry **Protoceratops** mother tried her best to defend her nest.

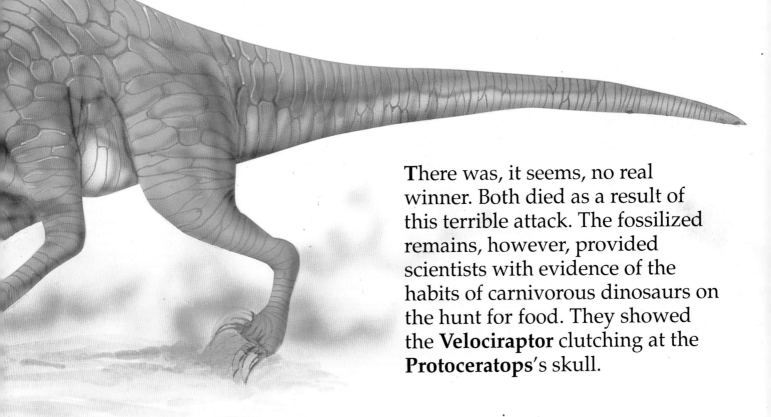

There was, it seems, no real winner. Both died as a result of this terrible attack. The fossilized remains, however, provided scientists with evidence of the habits of carnivorous dinosaurs on the hunt for food. They showed the **Velociraptor** clutching at the **Protoceratops**'s skull.

Vicious killer

Scientists believe that **Velociraptor** probably hunted for food in small packs. When they spotted a likely victim, they raced up to it, chasing it if it tried to run away. If it tried to defend itself, the **Velociraptor** pranced around, keeping just out of range of the victim's butting head and lashing tail until the creature being chased grew tired.

When a **Velociraptor** was close enough to attack, it lunged forward in order to grab its prey's head with grasping fingers. Then, standing on one leg and balancing with its long, stiff tail, **Velociraptor** slashed cruelly at the victim's soft undersides with the huge, curved, knifelike claw on its second toe, tearing at the flesh.

The victim's back may have been protected by bony lumps and leathery skin, but its belly was probably soft and easily ripped by the **Velociraptor**'s vicious claw.

Snapping its long jaws, **Velociraptor** would bite and tear at the victim's head and neck with its sharp teeth.

Once **Velociraptor** had a good grip with its jaws, the victim could not pull away from **Velociraptor**'s curved teeth, however hard it tried. When **Velociraptor** sank its teeth and claws into its prey, the victim rarely escaped without dreadful injuries.

Velociraptor and family

They all had slim bodies; long, curved claws; sharp teeth; and long, thin tails.

4

Velociraptor (1) belonged to a group or family of dinosaurs called **Dromaeosaurids** (<u>DROME</u>-EE-OH-<u>SAW</u>-RIDS). All the members of this group were fast and fearsome hunters that relied on killing other dinosaurs for food.

2

3

One of the larger members of the family was **Deinonychus** (DIE-NO-NIKE-US) **(2)**. Its name means "terrible claw" because there was a huge claw on its second toe. The animal walked and ran on its long third and fourth toes, holding up its long, stiff tail. **Deinonychus** lived in what is now the western United States before **Velociraptor** evolved.

Another cousin of this fierce family was **Dromaeosaurus** (DROME-EE-OH-SAW-RUS) **(3)**. Its name means "running reptile."

Dromaeosaurus was about the same size as **Velociraptor** and was very similar to the rest of the family. It lived 90 million years ago in what is now Alberta, Canada.

Scientists have found the bones of several dinosaurs that they think are also cousins of **Velociraptor**. One from Mongolia is called **Hulsanpes** (HULL-SAN-PEZ), meaning "foot from Khulsan" because all that has been found is its back foot.

Like **Velociraptor**, it, too, was a small, two-legged predator.

Utahraptor (YOO-TAH-RAP-TOR) **(4)** is an exciting new dinosaur find. It was discovered in 1992 in eastern Utah in the United States.

1

Utahraptor grew to 23 feet (7 m) long and had very sharp claws on its hands and feet.

Velociraptor data

Velociraptor was a small, speedy dinosaur. It held its head up as it hunted, always on the lookout for a meal. It was strong and agile. Although small, it was a fierce hunter.

Grabbing claws

Velociraptor had three very strong fingers on its long, powerful arms that ended in long, sharp claws. When it was close enough, **Velociraptor** would grab at its prey with its claws, digging them in and holding on tightly.

Slashing feet

Velociraptor had four clawed toes on each foot. It walked and ran on the third and fourth toes. The second toe had a special claw.

It looked just like the one above and could be lifted back off the ground. The first toe was much smaller and faced backward.

Useful tail

This dinosaur had a long, thin tail. **Velociraptor** held its tail up to balance its body when running.

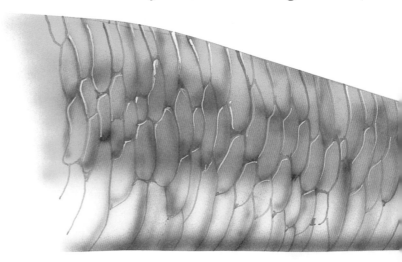

Narrow head

Velociraptor had a long, narrow head with a flat snout. It had large sockets for its eyes, which means it probably had big eyes and good eyesight. Scientists have found that its brain was much larger than those of most dinosaurs, so it was probably very intelligent.

Velociraptor also used it for balance when attacking. **Velociraptor** would prop itself up on its tail, leaving one back leg free to stab at its victim.

Razor teeth

Velociraptor had rows of teeth in its long, narrow jaws. The teeth were long and sharp, and they curved backward. **Velociraptor** used its teeth to bite and kill its prey.

GLOSSARY

carnivores — meat-eating animals.

evolve — to change or develop gradually from one form to another.

expedition — a journey or voyage.

fossils — traces or remains of plants and animals found in rock.

herbivores — plant-eating animals.

mammals — warm-blooded animals that nurse their young with milk from their own bodies. Mammals always have some hair or fur on their bodies.

pack — a group of similar or related animals.

plains — large, flat, treeless areas of land.

predators — animals that kill other animals for food.

prey — animals that are killed for food by other animals.

remains — a dead body or corpse.

snout — protruding nose and jaws of an animal.

INDEX

24